Communicate!

Sports
Speeches

Ben Nussbaum

Publishing Credits

Rachelle Cracchiolo, M.S.Ed., *Publisher*
Conni Medina, M.A.Ed., *Managing Editor*
Nika Fabienke, Ed.D., *Series Developer*
June Kikuchi, *Content Director*
John Leach, *Assistant Editor*
Evan Ferrell, *Graphic Designer*

Image Credits: front cover Focus on Sport/Getty Images; p.20 Aaron Josefczyk/Reuters/Newscom; p.21 Eric Espada/Cal Sport Media/Newscom; p.22 A.Ricardo/Shutterstock; p.23 Nelson Ching/Bloomberg via Getty Images; p.23 (bottom) Vastram/Shutterstock; p.24 (bottom) dasfx32/Shutterstock; pp.24–25 AP Photo; p.26 Bill Greenblatt/UPI/Newscom; p.27 Bettmann/Getty Images; pp.28–29 Lev Radin/Shutterstock; pp.30–31 Stephen Lew/Sportswire/Newscom; p.32 (bottom) Natursports/Shutterstock; pp.32–33 Alonzo Adams/USA Today Sports/Newscom; pp.34–35 Library of Congress [LC-DIG-hec-22989]; p.35 (bottom) Pictorial Press Ltd/Alamy; p.36 Public Domain; p.37 (bottom) Eliot Elisofon/The LIFE Picture Collection/Getty Images; p.38 (bottom left), p. 41 (bottom) Everett Collection/Newscom; p.38 (bottom right) Tony Donaldson/Icon SMI/Newscom; pp.40–41 Scott Woodham Photography/Shutterstock; all other images from iStock and/or Shutterstock.

Library of Congress Cataloging-in-Publication Data

Names: Nussbaum, Ben, 1975- author.
Title: Communicate! : sports speeches / Ben Nussbaum.
Description: Huntington Beach, CA : Teacher Created Materials, 2019. | Includes bibliographical references and index. | Audience: Grade 7 to 8.
Identifiers: LCCN 2017056447 (print) | LCCN 2018010927 (ebook) | ISBN 9781425850050 (e-book) | ISBN 9781425850067 (pbk. : alk. paper)
Subjects: LCSH: Sports--Quotations, maxims, etc.--Juvenile literature. | Athletes--Quotations--Juvenile literature.
Classification: LCC GV707 (ebook) | LCC GV707 .N87 2019 (print) | DDC 796--dc23
LC record available at https://lccn.loc.gov/2017056447

Teacher Created Materials

5301 Oceanus Drive
Huntington Beach, CA 92649-1030
www.tcmpub.com

ISBN 978-1-4258-5006-7

© 2019 Teacher Created Materials, Inc.

Table of Contents

The Champ

In 1964, Cassius Clay prepared to fight Sonny Liston, the reigning heavyweight boxing champion. Clay announced that he would "float like a butterfly, sting like a bee." Even though he was an underdog in the world of boxing, he predicted "the total eclipse of Sonny."

Liston surrendered at the start of the seventh round, making Clay the new champion and his prediction true. Still in the ring, Clay shouted, "I am the king of the world!"

"I'm a bad man," Clay exclaimed. Mobbed by supporters, he continued: "I shook up the world! … You must listen to me!" Before the fight, Clay was **cantankerous**, witty, and amusing. After the fight, raw with emotion, he was absolutely **mesmerizing**.

Days later, Clay changed his name to Muhammad Ali. He delivered many more memorable performances—as a boxer and as an **orator**. Ali's legend is proof that in the world of sports, words matter.

Not Lip Service

One of Clay's nicknames was the Louisville Lip, a reference to his nonstop chatter and his hometown of Louisville, Kentucky. Today, the city is home to a museum and multicultural center named after the boxer. Its motto is "Be great, do great things."

Cassius Clay

Sonny Liston

What a Stunt!

To convince Liston to fight him, Clay showed up outside Liston's house at three o'clock in the morning. Liston walked outside in his pajamas to get a good look at the challenger. Clay made sure journalists were on hand to see the whole thing.

Al Pacino in *Any Given Sunday*

Rock It, Rocky

Each *Rocky* movie includes inspiring speeches, but the most famous might be from *Rocky Balboa*, released in 2006. Sylvester Stallone plays the aging title character. "It ain't about how hard you hit," he says. "It's about how hard you can get hit and keep moving forward."

Magical Movie Moments

Some of the greatest sports speeches do not come from real-life athletes but rather from those portrayed in movies. These speeches, though penned by **screenwriters**, are inspiring, memorable, and have stood the test of time.

In *Any Given Sunday*, Al Pacino plays veteran football coach Tony D'Amato. After declaring that football and life are both games of inches, he says, "On this team, we fight for that inch. …I am still willing to fight and die for that inch, because that's what living is, the six inches in front of your face." It's a **rousing** speech with valuable life lessons.

Another quote-worthy fictional football coach is Eric Taylor from television's *Friday Night Lights*, played by Kyle Chandler. Taylor has a simple pre-game slogan he uses to motivate his team: "Clear eyes, full hearts, can't lose." These words inspire people off-screen as well. Other famous sports speeches are a mix of reality and legend.

A "Can't Lose" Tattoo

Connie Britton, one of the stars of *Friday Night Lights*, talked about the famous "Clear eyes, full hearts, can't lose" mantra in an interview. "I've had many people who've been struggling with cancer and other illnesses tell me that it's been something that's very impactful for them," she said. "A lot of people have it tattooed on them!"

The Gipper

"Win one for the Gipper" might be the most famous sports sound bite of all time. George Gipp played football for the University of Notre Dame between 1917 and 1920. Shortly after his senior season, he became ill and died. Coach Knute Rockne (noot RAHK-nee) was one of his last visitors in the hospital. In 1928, Rockne **invoked** Gipp's memory in a locker room speech. Rockne relayed to his players that Gipp, on his deathbed, had asked Rockne to tell the team to win a game in his memory. Inspired, Notre Dame beat the mighty U.S. Army team from West Point.

The 1940 movie *Knute Rockne, All American* amped up the story. The Hollywood version of Rockne delivers these poetic lines: "The last thing George said to me, 'Rock,' he said, 'sometime when the team is up against it and the breaks are beating the boys, tell them to go out there…and win just one for the Gipper.'"

President Gipp

Before Ronald Reagan was president, he was an actor. He portrayed Gipp in *Knute Rockne, All American*. One of Reagan's nicknames as president was "the Gipper." He sometimes asked voters to "win one for the Gipper."

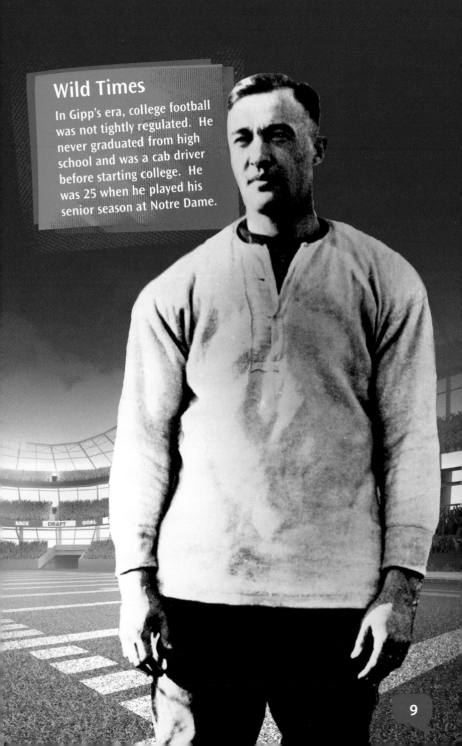

Wild Times

In Gipp's era, college football was not tightly regulated. He never graduated from high school and was a cab driver before starting college. He was 25 when he played his senior season at Notre Dame.

Many people think that the words in the movie are a direct quotation. However, it's not exactly clear what the real Rockne said, but players who heard his actual locker room speech about Gipp agree that it was much more direct and simple.

Rockne may have even made up the story about Gipp's last request as a motivational **ploy**. Gipp was not an emotional or sentimental person, according to his teammates. His friends thought it was unlikely he would have wanted the team to "win one for the Gipper."

A different element of Rockne's legend is also not completely accurate. One of his motivational talks is often replayed on television. "Fight, fight, fight, fight, fight!" the coach says, shaking his fists dramatically. The performance was filmed for a **newsreel** and doesn't relate to an actual football game. But many people think it is a real locker room speech.

"Five Foot Nothin'"

Rudy, another famous sports movie, tells the true story of a walk-on athlete at Notre Dame. Its most iconic lines come when a groundskeeper lectures Rudy about not quitting: "You're five foot nothin', a hundred and nothin', and hardly have a speck of athletic ability," he tells Rudy. "And you hung in with the best college football team in the land for two years."

Knute Rockne

Thinking Ahead

Under Rockne's guidance, Notre Dame won 105 games and only lost 12. He was an innovative coach who created new formations and plays. He was the first coach to travel widely with his team, taking the Indiana-based team to the East Coast and California for games.

A Great Opportunity

The movie *Miracle* tells the story of the Miracle on Ice, a hockey game between the United States and the Soviet Union played at the 1980 Winter Olympics. The Soviets were huge favorites but were **upset** by a determined and scrappy American team.

In the movie, Kurt Russell portrays coach Herb Brooks. He gives an inspiring locker room speech before the game: "Great moments are born from great opportunity. That's what you have here tonight, boys. That's what you've earned here tonight. …Tonight, we stay with them, and we shut them down because we can. Tonight, we are the greatest hockey team in the world."

The speech delivered in the movie was based on 20-year-old memories of what Brooks said that were then embellished by Hollywood **wordsmiths**. But these changes don't make Brooks's words or the U.S. victory any less inspiring!

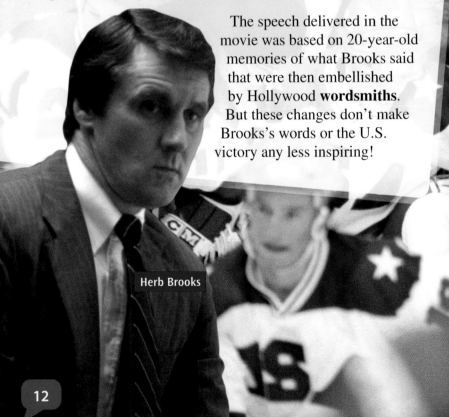

Herb Brooks

A Crazy Upset

How dominant were the Soviets? They beat the NHL All-Stars 6–0. They played the United States in an exhibition game right before the Olympics and won 10–3.

Kurt Russell as Herb Brooks in *Miracle*

Do You Believe?

Sports announcer Al Michaels called the 1980 Olympic hockey game on television. His description of the closing moments is legendary: "Five seconds left in the game. Do you believe in miracles? Yes!" he announced as the buzzer went off.

Great Calls

There are times when the action on the field and the sportscaster's words used to describe it blend into one incredible, memorable moment. Here are three of the most famous calls in sports history.

"There's nothing real in the world!"

A bizarre play ended an NFL game during the 1978 season. The ball was fumbled, then it bounced around the field and finally into the end zone, where a player fell on it for the winning touchdown.

Announcer Bill King described it this way: "The Oakland Raiders have scored on the most zany, unbelievable, absolutely impossible dream of a play. ...There's nothing real in the world anymore! The Raiders have won the football game!"

"The band is out on the field!"

During the 1982 college football season, Stanford took the lead over Cal on a late field goal. Stanford then kicked off with four seconds on the clock.

After a series of lateral passes and narrow escapes, a Cal player streaked toward the end zone. However, the Stanford band thought the game was over and entered the field, creating a confused mass of football players and band members.

Announcer Joe Starkey described the play: "They get it to Rodgers! They get it back now to the 30, they're down to the 20... oh, the band is out on the field! He's gonna go into the end zone! He got into the end zone!"

"The impossible has happened!"

In 1988, the Los Angeles Dodgers were expected to have a mediocre season at best. But the team surprised everyone when they wound up in the World Series.

In Game 1, the Dodgers were down 3–4 in the bottom of the ninth inning. An injured Kirk Gibson came to bat as a pinch hitter and hit a two-run home run. As Gibson circled the bases and pumped his fists, Vin Scully, the longtime Dodgers announcer, wrapped up the game poetically: "In a year that has been so improbable, the impossible has happened!"

The Dodgers went on to win the World Series, four games to one.

Pat Summitt

From the Bottom to the Summitt

Summitt was only 22 when she became the head coach at Tennessee. Women's sports were just becoming popular at the university level. In the early days of her career, she washed the team's uniforms and drove the team van to games.

Embracing the Grind

What makes a great athlete? Some would say effort and determination—both during the game and during practice. Many of the greatest sports speeches include wisdom and inspiration about working hard, never giving up, and having mental and physical toughness.

Pat Summitt won 1,098 games as the coach of the University of Tennessee women's basketball team. She expressed her philosophy in just a few words: "How am I going to beat you? I'm going to outwork you. That's it. That's all there is to it."

Legendary professional football coach Vince Lombardi expressed a related thought: "I've never known a man worth his salt who in the long run, deep down in his heart, didn't appreciate the grind, the discipline."

statue of Vince Lombardi

Is Winning Everything?

Vince Lombardi didn't coin the expression "Winning isn't everything, it's the only thing," but he did make it popular. Later in life, he said, "I wished I'd never said the thing. ...I meant having a goal. I sure didn't mean for people to crush human values and morality."

The Promise

Early in the 2008 college football season, the Florida Gators lost to the Ole Miss Rebels. Quarterback Tim Tebow (TEE-boh) was devastated. At a press conference following the loss, Tebow said, "I promise you one thing. A lot of good will come out of this."

He continued, "You will never see any player in the entire country play as hard as I will play the rest of the season. And you will never see someone push the rest of the team as hard as I will push everybody the rest of the season." He finished with, "You will never see a team play harder than we will the rest of the season."

After Tebow's passionate speech, Florida won the rest of its games and the national championship. Tebow's promise became part of college football **lore**.

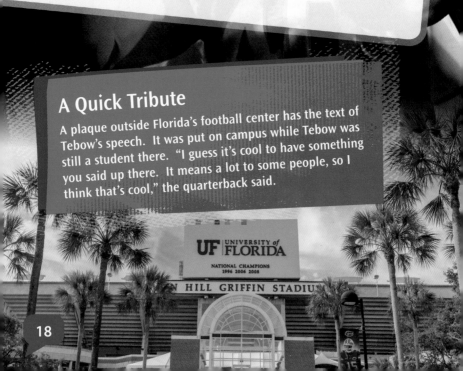

A Quick Tribute

A plaque outside Florida's football center has the text of Tebow's speech. It was put on campus while Tebow was still a student there. "I guess it's cool to have something you said up there. It means a lot to some people, so I think that's cool," the quarterback said.

UF | UNIVERSITY of FLORIDA

NATIONAL CHAMPIONS
1996 2006 2008

HILL GRIFFIN STADIU

Tim Tebow

No Time to Lose

Another memorable Tebow speech came at halftime of the 2009 BCS National Championship Game. During an emotional huddle, he pumped up his teammates. "We've got 30 minutes for the rest of our lives!" he told them, repeating, "We got 30 minutes!"

Full House

Irvin has 16 brothers and sisters. The family lived in a two-bedroom house, but his father converted the porch and garage into a third room. Irvin did not sleep in a bed by himself until college.

Michael Irvin

"Look Up, Get Up"

As a professional football player, Michael Irvin was known for his great plays on the field and his problems off the field. When he was inducted into the Pro Football Hall of Fame in 2007, his speech surprised many people. It was humble and inspiring, worthy of the Hall of Fame in every way.

He talked about a moment of pain when he was disappointed in his own behavior and full of self-doubt. He said, "My heart cried out, 'God, why must I go through so many peaks and valleys?'"

The crowd was **riveted**. Irvin went on: "At that moment, a voice came over me and said, 'Look up, get up, and don't ever give up. You tell everyone or anyone that has ever doubted, thought they did not measure up, or wanted to quit, you tell them to look up, get up, and don't ever give up.'"

Tearjerker

Cornerback Darrell Green gave a memorable speech when he was inducted into the Pro Football Hall of Fame in 2008. "You bet your life I'm going to cry. You bet your life I will," he said to start his emotional speech.

Words of Wisdom

The world of sports might seem like a strange place to look for wisdom, but dig a little deeper. Coaches try to **outmaneuver** each other with sophisticated strategies, while players need to think clearly to weather the roller-coaster ride of a long season. **Savvy** athletes win with their brains *and* their **brawn**.

The journey to excellence requires intelligence and knowing oneself. Ronda Rousey (ROW-zee) earned an Olympic medal in judo and is a mixed martial arts champion. "Everything I've learned from fighting, I've been able to apply to my life outside of it," she said.

Despite making a living in the ring, she said, "I'm scared all the time. You have to have fear in order to have courage. I'm a courageous person because I'm a scared person."

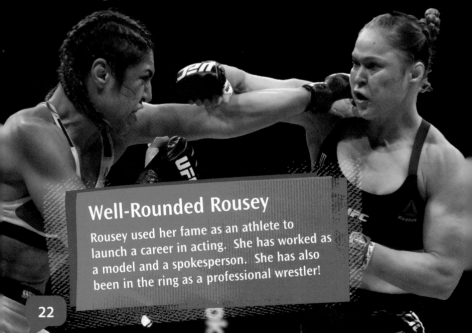

Well-Rounded Rousey

Rousey used her fame as an athlete to launch a career in acting. She has worked as a model and a spokesperson. She has also been in the ring as a professional wrestler!

Ronda Rousey

One Smart Guy

Ryan Fitzpatrick had a long career in the NFL as a quarterback. But he is best known as one of the smartest football players ever. The Harvard graduate and his eight-year-old son appeared in a viral video that showed each solving a Rubik's Cube puzzle in under two minutes.

A Forever Speech

College basketball coach Jim Valvano, better known as Jimmy V, was fighting cancer and had less than two months to live when he spoke at the 1993 ESPY Awards. He was accepting the Arthur Ashe Courage and Humanitarian Award.

"There are three things we all should do every day," Valvano said. "Number one is laugh—you should laugh every day. Number two is think—you should spend some time in thought. Number three is you should have your emotions moved to tears."

Valvano concluded by saying, "Cancer can take away all my physical ability. It cannot touch my mind, it cannot touch my heart, and it cannot touch my soul, and those three things are going to carry on forever."

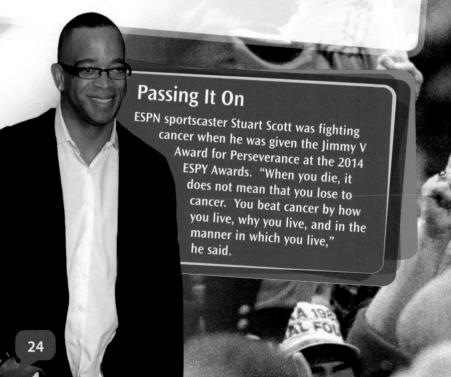

Passing It On

ESPN sportscaster Stuart Scott was fighting cancer when he was given the Jimmy V Award for Perseverance at the 2014 ESPY Awards. "When you die, it does not mean that you lose to cancer. You beat cancer by how you live, why you live, and in the manner in which you live," he said.

Doing Good

Valvano created the V Foundation for Cancer Research. The organization has spent more than $170 million on research. Many of Valvano's fellow coaches volunteer their time to help raise money.

Jim Valvano

"Make Things Better"

Roberto Clemente was a baseball player. When an earthquake struck Nicaragua in 1972, he sent food and clothes to the people there. When these supplies were stolen, Clemente decided to fly down with the next delivery. He wanted to make sure the aid made it to the people who needed it. The plane crashed into the ocean after takeoff, killing everyone on board.

After this tragedy, a speech that he had given the year before received fresh attention. "If you have an opportunity to accomplish something that will make things better for someone coming behind you and you don't do that, you are wasting your time on this Earth," Clemente had said.

Clemente is still a **revered** figure in baseball. His actions and his words made a powerful **legacy**.

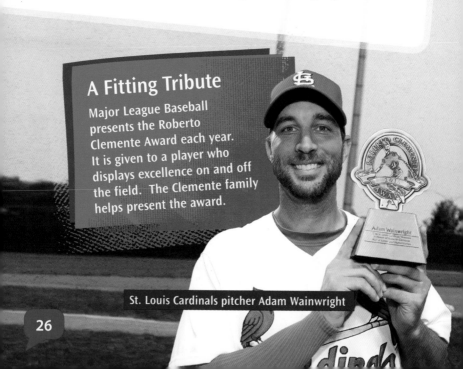

A Fitting Tribute

Major League Baseball presents the Roberto Clemente Award each year. It is given to a player who displays excellence on and off the field. The Clemente family helps present the award.

St. Louis Cardinals pitcher Adam Wainwright

Roberto Clemente

Roberto, not Bob

Clemente was one of the first Hispanic baseball stars, and he had to fight to be treated with respect. One way he did so was to insist on being called Roberto. Many journalists wanted to **anglicize** his name to Bob or Bobby.

Describing Messi

The winner of multiple *Ballon d'Or* trophies and one of the world's best soccer players, Lionel Messi of Argentina, sometimes defies description. Teammates, coaches, and journalists outdo each other finding new ways to describe his excellence. Here are some of the more colorful and eloquent ways Messi has been described.

"When he's on the ball, he opens a crack which we can peek through to spy on the essence of football."
—teammate Santi Solari

"If he is so good, how can you express that? The **superlatives** ran out ages ago. On these pages, swearing has been tried. Or perhaps a symbol, something to signify that we have gone beyond words now."
—journalist Sid Lowe

"I believe Leo comes from a marvelous planet, the one where exceptional people like violinists, architects, and doctors are created. The chosen people."
—Josep Maria Minguella, Messi's former agent

"He has **chromosomes** in his body that belong in a Bengal tiger, man!"
—commentator Ray Hudson

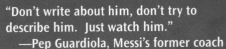

"Don't write about him, don't try to describe him. Just watch him."
—Pep Guardiola, Messi's former coach

"He plays a game with which we are not familiar."
—commentator Gary Lineker

"Nothing less than the equivalent of a footballing **bird of paradise**."
—commentator Ray Hudson

"Although he may not be human, it's good that Messi still thinks he is."
—teammate Javier Mascherano

Saying Thanks

Many successful athletes are known for their gratitude and **humility**.

While being inducted into the Pro Football Hall of Fame, Walter Payton said that he succeeded because of his team. He said coaches showed him "what hard work and determination would do if you put forth the effort and you take a little time." The Chicago Bears running back played for 13 seasons.

New Orleans Saints quarterback Drew Brees gave the world a great example of humility after he set the NFL record for passing yards in a season: "There may be only one name that goes in the record book, but it's all about you guys," he told his teammates. Brees kept the spotlight on them, saying, "You make me so proud."

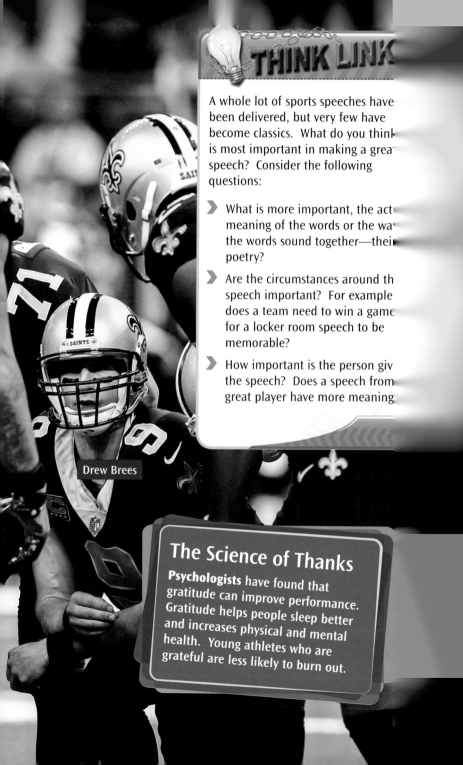

THINK LINK

A whole lot of sports speeches have been delivered, but very few have become classics. What do you think is most important in making a great speech? Consider the following questions:

❯ What is more important, the actual meaning of the words or the way the words sound together—their poetry?

❯ Are the circumstances around the speech important? For example, does a team need to win a game for a locker room speech to be memorable?

❯ How important is the person giving the speech? Does a speech from a great player have more meaning?

Drew Brees

The Science of Thanks

Psychologists have found that gratitude can improve performance. Gratitude helps people sleep better and increases physical and mental health. Young athletes who are grateful are less likely to burn out.

"The Real MVP"

In 2014, Kevin Durant was named the Most Valuable Player of the National Basketball Association (NBA). Even though he was a famous athlete and a millionaire many times over, he showed remarkable humility. In his acceptance speech, he thanked each of his teammates individually, with thoughtful remarks for each of them.

He saved the best for last, closing his speech with a moving tribute to his mother: "You put clothes on our backs, food on the table. When you didn't eat, you made sure we ate," he said. "You went to sleep hungry. You sacrificed for us," Durant said before concluding, "You're the real MVP."

The genuine, emotional, and wise speech was a huge hit, replayed over and over on social media.

A Rose for Mom

Three years earlier, a different NBA star put his mom in the headlines when he accepted the MVP award. Derrick Rose choked back tears as he called his mom "my heart, the reason why I play the way I play. Just everything."

Durant's epic thank-you speech motivated the Lifetime channel to make a movie about his mother. It was called *The Real MVP: The Wanda Durant Story*. It aired during Mother's Day weekend!

Durant celebrates a win with his mother.

The Luckiest Man

Lou Gehrig (GAIR-ihg) Appreciation Day took place on July 4, 1939, in Yankee Stadium. The great first baseman had benched himself earlier in the season because of weakness. Then, he was diagnosed with a fatal **degenerative** illness.

In the span of just weeks, he had gone from a superstar famous for his streak of playing in consecutive games to a sick, dying man. The crowd was somber as his teammates paid tribute to the slugger. At last, Gehrig walked to the microphone to deliver a short speech.

"For the past two weeks, you have been reading about a bad break I got. Today, I consider myself the luckiest man on the face of the Earth. I have been in ballparks for 17 years and have never received anything but kindness and encouragement," he said.

STOP! THINK...

Lou Gehrig was an amazing athlete.

▶ What can you infer about him based on the numbers below?

▶ Which fact is most surprising and why?

2,130: Gehrig played this many consecutive games, a record that stood until 1995.

$400: This is how much Gehrig's first professional contract paid him each month. That's about $5,700 today.

184: This was his runs batted in (RBI) total in 1931, still an American League record.

23: He had this many career grand-slam home runs, a record that stood until 2013.

1: A U.S. Navy ship was named after Gehrig. The SS *Lou Gehrig* was involved in World War II.

Babe's Turn

Gehrig was teammates with Babe Ruth, whom many consider to be the best baseball player of all time. In 1947, Ruth, fatally ill, gave his own farewell speech at Yankee Stadium. "The only real game, I think, in the world is baseball," Ruth said.

Fighting ALS

Gehrig died of a disease called *amyotrophic lateral sclerosis*, also known as ALS. In 2014, the "Ice Bucket Challenge" went viral. It was a social media campaign to raise money to fight ALS.

Gehrig's voice echoed around the stadium as he continued. He thanked his managers and the Yankees executives and praised his parents and his mother-in-law. He marveled at the outpouring of kindness shown to him. "When the New York Giants, a team you would give your right arm to beat, and vice versa, sends you a gift—that's something."

Gehrig finished by saying, "I may have had a tough break, but I have an awful lot to live for." This speech might be the most famous in all of sports. Gehrig responded to an incredible personal tragedy with humility, grace, and **eloquence**.

In 1939, the Yankees retired Gehrig's number, 4. His was the first number retired in baseball history. When Gehrig died two years later, he was mourned as a national hero.

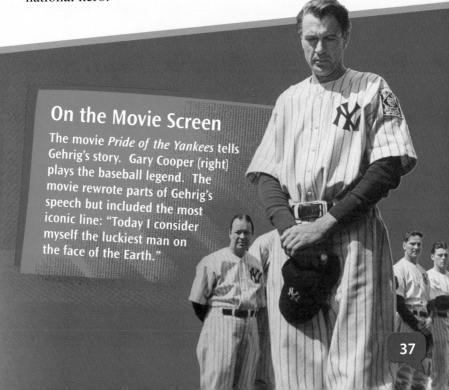

On the Movie Screen

The movie *Pride of the Yankees* tells Gehrig's story. Gary Cooper (right) plays the baseball legend. The movie rewrote parts of Gehrig's speech but included the most iconic line: "Today I consider myself the luckiest man on the face of the Earth."

Who Said It?

Yogi Berra was a great baseball player. But he's most famous for his Yogiisms—unique expressions that seem nonsensical or obvious but often have hidden depth. A classic Yogiism is "You can observe a lot by just watching."

John Wooden was a legendary basketball coach at the University of California, Los Angeles, for almost 30 years. While Berra's most famous quotations were delivered off the cuff, Wooden's kernels of wit and wisdom were carefully crafted. They're elegant and concise. They often include advice about working hard and being unselfish. A classic Woodenism is "Never mistake activity for achievement."

Take a look at the following quotations. Each is either a classic Yogiism or Woodenism. Who do you think said each one?

Yogi Berra

John Wooden

Yogi or Wooden?

1. "The future ain't what it used to be."

2. "The main ingredient of stardom is the rest of the team."

3. "You can't let praise or criticism get to you. It's a weakness to get caught up in either one."

4. "I never said most of the things I said."

5. "I always thought that record would stand until it was broken."

6. "Winning takes talent, to repeat takes character."

7. "You should always go to other people's funerals. Otherwise, they won't come to yours."

8. "We made too many wrong mistakes."

9. "Things turn out best for the people who make the best of the way things turn out."

10. "Don't measure yourself by what you have accomplished, but by what you should have accomplished with your ability."

Berra: 1, 4, 5, 7, 8   Wooden: 2, 3, 6, 9, 10

The Recipe

By 1972, Muhammad Ali was one of the most famous athletes in the world, controversial and beloved in equal measure, with hard-earned wisdom from almost a decade in the spotlight. When a television interviewer asked how he wanted to be remembered, Ali responded:

"I would like for them to say, 'He took a few cups of love. He took one tablespoon of patience, one teaspoon of generosity, one pint of kindness; he took one quart of laughter, one pinch of concern, and then he mixed willingness with happiness. He added lots of faith, and he stirred it up well. Then he spread it over a span of a lifetime, and he served it to each and every deserving person he met.'"

The room burst into applause as the champion grinned. It was a classic Ali performance, and he hadn't even used his fists.

An Epic Showdown

In 1978, DC Comics published a special-edition comic book. In the book, Muhammad Ali and Superman team up to fight aliens who are invading Earth. They also box each other. Ali emerges victorious.

The Odd Couple

Ali had a special relationship with broadcaster Howard Cosell. The two men were equally opinionated. They were must-see television when they were together. Cosell once said, "You're being extremely **truculent**." Ali replied, "Whatever truculent means, if that's good, I'm that."

Glossary

anglicize—to change a word or name to English

bird of paradise—a type of bird known for its bright and colorful plumage

brawn—muscular strength

cantankerous—difficult and argumentative, sometimes in an amusing way

chromosomes—structures in cells that contain genes

degenerative—causing something to become weaker or less functional over time

eloquence—the ability to speak or write convincingly

humility—the quality of being humble

invoked—mentioned in an attempt to make people feel a certain way

legacy—something that comes from someone in the past

lore—a body of knowledge or tradition

mesmerizing—fascinating; impossible to put down or turn away from

newsreel—short movies about current events that were shown in theaters

orator—someone who is known for skill at public speaking

outmaneuver—to win or gain an advantage over using clever strategies

ploy—a trick or clever strategy

psychologists—people who study the human mind

revered—respected very much

riveted—rapt with attention

rousing—giving rise to excitement

savvy—having practical understanding or knowledge of something

screenwriters—people who write movies and television shows

superlatives—admiring expressions of praise

truculent—feeling or displaying eagerness to fight

upset—defeated unexpectedly

wordsmiths—skillful writers

Index

Check It Out!

Books

Christopher, Matt. 2015. *Great Americans in Sports: Drew Brees*. Little, Brown Books for Young Readers.

Editors of Sports Illustrated Kids. 2017. *Big Book of WHO Baseball*. Sports Illustrated.

Finch, Jennie. 2011. *Throw Like a Girl: How to Dream Big & Believe in Yourself*. Triumph Books.

Gutman, Dan. 2012. *Roberto & Me*. HarperCollins.

Smith, Charles R., Jr. 2010. *12 Rounds to Glory: The Story of Muhammad Ali*. Candlewick.

Websites

Muhammad Ali Center. www.alicenter.org.

John Wooden. www.coachwooden.com.

V Foundation. www.jimmyv.org.

Muhammad Ali. www.muhammadali.com.

Yogi Berra Museum and Learning Center. www.yogiberramuseum.org.

Movies

Anspaugh, David. *Rudy*. 1993. TriStar Pictures.

Bacon, Lloyd. *Knute Rockne, All American*. 1940. Warner Bros. Pictures.

O'Connor, Gavin. *Miracle*. 2004. Walt Disney Pictures.

Wood, Sam. *Pride of the Yankees*. 1942. Samuel Goldwyn Productions.

Try It!

Some of the best sports speeches are given at awards ceremonies where athletes are honored in front of their peers. Imagine that at a school assembly, you will accept an award and make a speech.

Answer these questions, and then use your answers to write a speech.

- Whom will you thank? What will you say about them?
- What do you want people to learn about you?
- Can you use the occasion to make a positive change in some way, perhaps by honoring someone who is underappreciated?

As you write your speech, keep these tips in mind:

- Read aloud what you've written. Some sentences might look good on paper but sound awkward when said aloud.
- Use a mix of long and short sentences.
- Find a good balance of serious and humorous things to say.
- Start and end on high notes.

About the Author

Ben Nussbaum lives in Arlington, Virginia, with his wife and two children, as well as a red fish and a white cat. He was the founding editor of *USA Today*'s special projects division. He's edited a book on NASCAR, a magazine on Muhammad Ali, and a newspaper special edition on college basketball, among many other projects. He's written dozens of books and is a full-time freelancer and consultant. He grew up in Indiana. His favorite sports movie is *Hoosiers*.